Waiting For
My Life

by LINDA PASTAN

Waiting For
My Life

Poems by

LINDA PASTAN

W · W · NORTON & COMPANY · NEW YORK · LONDON

I would like to thank the following periodicals in which many of these poems first appeared: *Antaeus; The Atlantic; The Bennington Review; The Carolina Quarterly; Confrontation; Field; Georgia Review; The Grecourt Review; Harper's Magazine; The Hudson Review; MSS; The Nation; The New England Quarterly; New Letters; New Republic; The New Yorker; Ploughshares; Poet Lore; Poetry; Prairie Schooner; Tennessee Poetry Miscellany; Three Rivers Poetry Journal; Thunder Mountain Review; Virginia Quarterly Review*. Four of these poems first appeared in a pamphlet titled *Even As We Sleep*, Croissant & Company, 1980. The poems *25th Anniversary* (1979) and *In Back Of* (1978) copyrighted © in the years shown by The New Yorker Magazine, Inc. I would like to thank the Maryland Arts Council for their support.

Published simultaneously in Canada by George J. McLeod Limited, Toronto.
Printed in the United States of America
First Edition

Library of Congress Cataloging in Publication Data

Pastan, Linda, 1932–
Waiting for my life. Poems.

I. Title.
PS3566.A775W3 1981   811'.54   80–20012
ISBN 0–393–01441–X
ISBN 0–393–00049–4 (pbk.)

W. W. Norton & Company, Inc. 500 Fifth Avenue, New York, N.Y. 10110
W. W. Norton & Company Ltd. 25 New Street Square, London EC4A 3NT

1 2 3 4 5 6 7 8 9 0

For my mother and
in memory of my father

Contents

3 ❦ The Verdict of Snow 51

Waiting For

My Life

Epilogue

Years later the girl died
no longer a girl,
and the old man fishing
in sullied waters
saw his one mistake
flash by—
but only for a moment.
The moon continued
its periodic rise and fall,
sometimes the shape
of a snow elk's horn,
sometimes a vague
repository of light.
Katerina married
someone else.
Robert, though only a minor character
grew into the hero
of another story.
And the house was rebuilt
by strangers.
Only the lake stayed the same,
its surface equivocal
as the pages of a book
on which everything remains
to be written.

Prologue

Nothing has happened yet.
The house settles
into its stones,
unoccupied;
the road curves
towards something—
away from something else.
A single elk bends
to the lake to drink,
or in the confusion of dusk
perhaps it is simply
an old tree
leaning over the water.
If there were voices,
their language would be
expectancy; but the silence
is nearly perfect.
Even the sun is motionless
before it takes that definite plunge
into the darkness
of the first chapter.

1

Friday's Child

Dreams

Dreams are the only
afterlife we know;
the place where the children
we were
rock in the arms of the children
we have become.

They are as many as leaves
in their migrations,
as birds whose deaths we learn of
by the single feather
left behind: a clue,
a particle of sleep

caught in the eye.
They are as irretrievable as sand
when the sea creeps up
its long knife glittering
in its teeth
to claim its patrimony.

Sometimes my father
in knickers and cap
waits on that shore,
the dream of him
a wound
not even morning can heal.

The dog's legs pump
in his sleep;
your closed eyelids flicker
as the reel unwinds:
watcher and watched,
archer and bull's-eye.

Last night I dreamed a lover in my arms
and woke innocent.
The sky was starry to the very rind,
his smile still burning there
like the tail of a comet
that has just blazed by.

McGuffey's First
Eclectic Reader

The sun is up
the sun is always up.
The silent "e"
keeps watch;
and 26 strong stones
can build a wall of syllables
for Nell and Ned
and Ann:

Rab was such a good dog,
Mother. We left him
under the big tree
by the brook
to take care of the dolls
and the basket.

But Rab has run away.
The basket's gone back to reeds
through which the night wind
blows; and mother was erased;
the dolls are painted harlots
in the Doll's Museum.

Where did it go, Rose?
I don't know;
away off, somewhere.

The fat hen
has left the nest.

I hand my daughter
this dusty book.
Framed in her window
the sky darkens to slate:
a lexicon of wandering stars.
Listen, child—the barking
in the distance
is Rab the dog star
trotting home
for dinner.

Friday's Child

We always called Cassandra
immature—the way she ran
through town with her electric hair
and torn clothes, telling us
what we already knew:
that regiments of clouds
were being formed
that could bombard us soon
with snow, could bury us;
that art is an equivocal gift;
that every flower awaited
its proper place
on our funeral wreaths.
We knew all that—
she was our own child.
But once betrothed to grief
what could we do but mourn?
We let her speak; and speak.
All words, anyway
are epitaphs.

Secrets

The secrets I keep
from myself
are the same secrets
the leaves keep
from the old trunk
of the tree
even as they turn
color.

They are the garbled
secrets
of the waterfall
about to be stunned
on rock;
the sound of the stream's
dry mouth
after weeks of drought.

Hush, says the nurse
to the new child howling
its one secret
into the world,
hush
as she buries
its mouth
in milk.

On the hearth the fire consumes
its own burning tongue,
I cannot read the ash.
By the gate
the trumpet flower sings
only silence
from its shapely
throat.

At night
I fall asleep
to the whippoorwill's
raucous lullabye,
old as the first garden:
never tell
never tell
never tell.

The Vanishing Point

As if you were the parent
and I the child
you patiently explain
perspective:
a pencilled dot
drawn on a picture plane
where parallel lines
converge—as if
that were as possible
as holding two kite strings
in one hand
the way you tried to do
on windy afternoons.

Still, I understand
that dot, that point
the eye drifts towards
on any horizon, the place
where all things lost
converge: the hairpins
your father took slowly
from my piled up hair
the night we met;
your face at five or seven;
and someone else—a voice
I almost listened to once—
who never asked again.

Letter to a Son at Exam Time

May again
and poems leaf out
from this old typewriter
shading the desk in half-light.
You at a college desk study different poems,
hold them warily by their dry stems—
so many leaves pressed to death
in a heavy book.

When you forget again
to call
it's poet and parent both
that you deny.
This is what I didn't know
I knew.

You woke up
on the wrong side
of my life.
For years I counted myself to sleep
on all the ways I might lose you:
death in its many-colored coat lounged
at the schoolhouse door, delivered
the milk, drove the carpool.

Now I catalogue leaves instead
on a weeping cherry.
It doesn't really weep,
nor do poets cry, so amazed
they are at the prosody
of pain.

You have a way with words yourself
you never asked for.
Though you disguise them
as best you can
in Gothic misspellings
there they stand in all their new muscle.
You will use them against me perhaps,
but you will use them.

may apples

last month a thousand
green parachutes opened
colonizing our deepest woods

may apples
you called them
though it was april then

now under every leafy eave
one white globe hangs
suburban as any porch lamp

lighting
what little wilderness
is left

Dress Rehearsal

In Thornton Wilder's Our Town
my own daughter playing Emily asked
"Do any humans ever realize life . . . ?"
The fresh-skinned boy who calls
too late each night,
playing the stage manager replied
"The saints and poets, maybe—they do some."
For a while after that I saw
my daughter in a circle of light
that seemed to follow her
even when she left the stage,
and pictured her veiled and married,
pictured a shovel seeking out a grave.
I stared at every new leaf
seeing as in a speeded-up film
the history of its changing colors
revealed in infant green.
Unreconciled to so much light
I drew the curtains early
and sent my daughter early to bed.

All Night

The children have gone
through doors so small
we may not follow
even if we stoop

and the dogs bark all night
hearing calls
in registers too high
for our frail senses.

We follow words instead
but they are only signposts
leading to other words
leaving us lost

in our own landscape.
We struggle merely to see
for the sun too has slipped away,
hiding its tracks

in afterlight,
to a place of unimagined
reds and golds
a place where children

lounge on grass
calling to dogs whose barking
they can still hear
all these years from home.

The One-Way Mirror Back

1.

The pages of my books
rustled
with the same sound
my mother's skirts made
on her way
out the door.

And my father's mustache
bobbed
in the distance
like the old rowboat
across the lake—
only a bit absurd,
only a little dangerous.

2.

I didn't have a brother,
though long before me
there was a baby
they never speak of
for whom I named
my son.

And when it became clear
I would not catch the ball
or cut into the frog
they forgave me again
because I was just
a girl.

3.

I hoarded A's at school
the way I hoarded aces
when I beat my mother
at Gin. There was tea
for my sore throat and honey
and light the color
of tea and honey.

On the radio Stella Dallas
talked of her beautiful
daughter Lolly
in almost the voice
my mother used
to tell my father
how many games I'd won.

4.

the small glow
of the flowers we called
japanese lanterns

swinging
on their long stems
lit the summer dusk

later the countryside blew by
the back seat of the car
as we sang rounds

my father's voice
my mother's voice
mine

row your boat . . .
oh how lovely is the evening . . .
merrily, merrily

our three voices braiding
braiding
into one voice

5.

shut up
I playfully
told my father
once
and he did
for seven long
days

6.

One day I knew
the simplicities
of power, a lesson
the leaf learns
when it breaks
through its chrysalis
of bark, a lesson
the sap learns
rising
through all the laws
of gravity.
I learned this lesson
late.

7.

What I remember
hardly happened;
what they say happened
I hardly remember.
In the one-way mirror back
I see only that appetite
was harder to appease
than hunger, dreams
more persistent
than appetite, tripping
me down their drowsy stairs
until I rested
in my nest of bones
unhurt.

Elegy

Somewhere a poem
is waiting for me
to write it: in the jewelry box,
coiled into an old ring
or stopping the hands
of a watch;
in the vanishing barn, risen
to the top of the pail
to be skimmed off;
or in the tree outside
engraved in green ink
on the underside of a leaf.

In my old room
the white curtains blow
like ghosts of themselves
over the sill;
under the bed misplaced words gather
to grab my helpless ankle.
It is a poem
the child I was hides
in the ear of the woman
I have become: a poem
whose lines were the lines
of my father's face.

Waiting For My Life

I waited for my life to start
for years, standing at bus stops
looking into the curved distance
thinking each bus was the wrong bus;
or lost in books where I would travel
without luggage from one page
to another; where the only breeze
was the rustle of pages turning,
and lives rose and set
in the violent colors of suns.

Sometimes my life coughed and coughed:
a stalled car about to catch,
and I would hold someone in my arms,
though it was always someone else I wanted.
Or I would board any bus, jostled
by thighs and elbows that knew
where they were going; collecting scraps
of talk, setting them down like bird song
in my notebook, where someday I would go
prospecting for my life.

2

The War Between
Desire And Dailiness

In Back Of

"I'm looking for things back of re-
marks that are said . . ."

William Stafford

In back of "I love you"
stands "goodbye."
In back of
"goodbye"
stands "it was lovely
there in the grass, drenched
in so much green
together."
Words that wait
are dark as shadows
in the back rooms
of mirrors:
when you raise
your right hand
in greeting,
they raise their left
in farewell.

Eyes Only

Dear lost sharer
of silences,
I would send a letter
the way the tree sends messages
in leaves,
or the sky in exclamations
of pure cloud.

Therefore I write
in this blue
ink, color
of secret veins
and arteries.
It is morning here.
Already the postman walks

the innocent streets,
dangerous as Aeolus
with his bag of winds,
or Hermes, the messenger,
god of sleep and dreams
who traces my image
upon this stamp.

In public buildings
letters are weighed
and sorted like meat;
in railway stations
huge sacks of mail
are hidden like robbers' booty
behind freight-car doors.

And in another city
the conjurer
will hold a fan of letters
before your outstretched hand—
"Pick any card . . ."
You must tear the envelope
as you would tear bread.

Only then dark rivers
of ink will thaw
and flow
under all the bridges
we have failed
to build
between us.

Excursion

I am a tourist
in my own life,
gazing at the exotic shapes
of flowers
as if someone else
had planted them;
barred
from the half lit rooms
of children
by an invisible
velvet rope.
The dresses in my closet
are costumes
for a different woman,
though I hide myself
in their silky textures.
The man asleep
in my bed
knows me best
in the dark.

Meditation By The Stove

I have banked the fires
of my body
into a small but steady blaze,
here in the kitchen
where the dough has a life of its own,
breathing under its damp cloth
like a sleeping child;
where the real child plays under the table,
pretending the tablecloth is a tent,
practicing departures; where a dim
brown bird dazzled by light
has flown into the windowpane
and lies stunned on the pavement—
it was never simple, even for birds,
this business of nests.
The innocent eye sees nothing, Auden says,
repeating what the snake told Eve,
what Eve told Adam, tired of gardens,
wanting the fully lived life.
But passion happens like an accident.
I could let the dough spill over the rim
of the bowl, neglecting to punch it down,
neglecting the child who waits under the table,
the mild tears already smudging her eyes.
We grow in such haphazard ways.
Today I feel wiser than the bird.
I know the window shuts me in,
that when I open it
the garden smells will make me restless.
And I have banked the fires of my body
into a small domestic flame for others
to warm their hands on for a while.

Who Is It Accuses Us?

Who is it accuses us of safety,
as if the family were soldiers
instead of hostages,
as if the gardens were not mined
with explosive peonies,
as if the most common death
were not by household accident?
We have chosen the dangerous life.
Consider the pale necks of the children
under their colored head scarves,
the skin around the husbands' eyes, flayed
by guilt and promises.
You who risk no more than your own skins
I tell you household Gods
are jealous Gods.
They will cover your window sills
with the dust of sunsets;
they will poison your secret wells
with longing.

What We Want

What we want
is never simple.
We move among the things
we thought we wanted:
a face, a room, an open book
and these things bear our names—
now they want us.
But what we want appears
in dreams, wearing disguises.
We fall past,
holding out our arms
and in the morning
our arms ache.
We don't remember the dream,
but the dream remembers us.
It is there all day
as an animal is there
under the table,
as the stars are there
even in full sun.

The Japanese Way

Now I have been caught
in the karma of past lives . . .

Kenrei Mon-in Ukyo no Diabu,
12th Century

In this eastern light
I feel my eyes
slant shut. I kneel
on tatami at your feet
and with delicate
gestures of wood
take crab from claw
to feed you. How easy
to hide in the sleeves
of a kimona, to feel
the silk seduce
my very skin,
to let my strong sons
be my only measure:
mother and wife—
as when you hold me here
and I can see
in the raked sand
all the ocean I need.
But over the nightingale floor
made cunningly so the wood
sings at the joints
when enemies approach,
I hear instead my sisters
tiptoe near, freeing
their complicated wings
of hair.

Attempt At Dialogue

"a hen telling the time is a sign of
bad luck"

Japanese proverb

I am the left-handed drinker
(drunkard, you call it)
who pours my own sake,
though only a thimbleful.

I am the Yama no Kami
who lifts my eyes
to my husband's—
to contradict him.

I am the poet
who sees in the falling plum leaves
all the places the wind
might take them.

"It's a cold
and western wind," you answer
"and our walls are made
of rice paper."

Elsewhere

Like a Shabbos Goy
I turn the lights on and off
so that somebody else
may speak with God.
Or like a young squire
I polish the armour with steel wool
and sharpen the pure
blade of a sword
for other people's battles.
At the doorway
your kiss brushes my mouth
like the wing of a bird
whose feathers
will be used elsewhere
for arrows, for pens,
for prophecy.

Hippolyte At Breakfast

She has forgotten
where her daughters leave off
and she begins,
so when they frown
she feels her jaw
turn to stone,
her mouth straightens into a line
the father may not cross.

They rise
from the table together
her daughters and she
shaking the crumbs
from the cloth,
shaking the cloth
like a flag
in the father's face.

And he scurries off,
a man hiding
behind the morning news,
a man who slips back
into the world
as if he were a swimmer
and the world
a stream.

The house settles
into its stays,
closing comfortably
behind him. Brooms tsk tsk,
curtains swell in the breeze,
and the din of pots and pans
can be heard—a distant artillery
all the way into town.

The War Between Desire And Dailiness

(Variation on a line by Robert Hass)

When you said "I think
I know your mind,"
you touched me
in the one private place
left. The heat
of those words ignites
my face, declares
a war between desire
and dailiness.
At the site of such longing
all order disappears.
I must summon arms:
spoons in the fists
of children, each beating
its own martial measure;
dates on the calendar marked
in blood for births, for deaths;
my only flag, a pillowcase
bleaching in the sun
on which no lover's head
has rested yet.
In the first moments of spring
I too am threatened
by thaw, deep underground.
Spring is the shortest season.
Let dailiness win.

By the Mailbox

The message you send me
is silence. It is a message
I try to understand
the way the roots
of trees must understand
the mitigating silence of water.
We take from nature
what we can. I study
the silences of stars, of stones.
I picture you miles north
leaning over the empty page.
Dear . . . you want to write.
But already the page is a window
curtained in the early silence
of snow.

Helen Bids Farewell
To Her Daughter Hermione

There is time
before I go
to mention the lily flowering
by the door—
how, when divided,
it multiplies.
I'm speaking now
of love.

There is time
to tell you
the only story I know:
a youth sets out,
a man or woman returns,
the rest is simply incident
or weather

and yet what storms
I could describe
swirling
in every thumbprint.

There is time
before I go
to show you the way
light slants
across a page
or through a doorway,
as if the darkness too
were vulnerable.

apologia

what we shared
was fever
call it what you will
the disoriented flesh
dreaming
of transformations
as the spark dreams
it has become
a flake of snow
even as it ignites
the house

Returning

She re-enters her life
The way a parachutist re-enters
the coarser atmosphere of earth,
exchanging the sensual shapes of clouds
for cloud-shaped trees rushing
to meet her, their branches sharp,
their soft leaves transitory.

She notices smells,
the scent of pines piercing
the surface of memory—
that dark lake submerged in pines
in which her husband
starts to swim
back into sight.

And as she lands
in their own garden,
after her brief but brilliant flight,
she pushes the silky parachute from her
as she pushed the white sheet
from her breasts
just yesterday.

When the Moment Is Over

When the moment is over—
the light we have turned inward
the way as children we press a flashlight
into our own flesh
making each limb seem
to smolder—
when that light goes off
we are saved once more
by dailiness:
the sun had continued
its unbroken journey;
the sheets may need smoothing
as the forehead needs smoothing
after fever.

What we have learned
we continue to learn
as we continually memorize objects
deep in our pockets: the key
to a certain door; a coin
whose severe face
is worn to a smile.
And we listen for echoes
from the buried chambers
of the heart
whose messages are tapped out
in unbreakable code,
whose fires are stoked secretly
even as we sleep.

Cold Front

The first cold front
is moving from the west
like a crusade
gathering forces
as it goes:
a grey phalanx
of rain, torn banners
of wind, the whole
rattle tattle army
of weather.
Now it is over
the Rockies, shaking
its fist of snow,
now over Kansas City—
a newspaper map charts
its battle course
in arrows.

Here, the still
languorous clouds
dream snow,
leaves flex
in the warm breeze
in preparation
for that final
flight,
that old refusal
of green.
We stockpile sweaters,
send the children off
to school, resolve
to hold through the day
the summer slogan

that only the day
matters.

Still, no death
is like another.
We must honor the season
by strict observance
of every tree.
Even as we step from the lake
for the last time,
armoured already
in gooseflesh,
even as we embrace,
I watch
over your shoulder
the last fireflies
kindle a flame
along the ivy—
it is our first
casualty.

Song

I am sick of the song
of the self,
that old melody
for one voice
running up and down
and up the scale
like a mouse maddened
by its own elusive
tail. I have heard that voice
shatter glass.

Nor do I ask
for martial music,
trumpets or drums
or the thoroughbass
of marching feet.
I long, instead, for bells
or for a simple trio: one bird
in the sycamore singing,
two birds in the oak
singing back.

3

The Verdict of Snow

after minor surgery

this is the dress rehearsal
when the body
like a constant lover
flirts for the first time
with faithlessness

when the body
like a passenger on a long journey
hears the conductor call out
the name
of the first stop

when the body
in all its fear and cunning
makes promises to me
it knows
it cannot keep

November

It is an old drama
this disappearance of the leaves,
this seeming death
of the landscape.
In a later scene,
or earlier,
the trees like gnarled magicians
produce handkerchiefs
of leaves
out of empty branches.

And we watch.
We are like children
at this spectacle
of leaves,
as if one day we too
will open the wooden doors
of our coffins
and come out smiling
and bowing
all over again.

A Middle-Aged Poet
Leaves the Movies

You come out weeping
for Iphegenia, for all our scrape-kneed
vulnerable daughters, only half innocent.
You travel the used-up streets,
back to the house where one day
the winds of your life suddenly
went slack
as Agamemnon had his usual way.

Now you turn to "larger" issues,
brushing aside the small poems of the self
as if they were so many gnats.
The tea has steeped to darkness
in your cup; the sun steeps at the edges
of the sky: the stuff of poems, you think—
and wrestle instead with the Greek alphabet.
From Troy only the women's tasks are left:

tomorrow you'll wrestle bread,
kneading it with your large hands,
letting it rise slowly in some dark place
the way the poems must slowy rise
through all your darknesses.
You'll write how Iphigenia once played
among the small but perfect Aegean flowers;
she never grew middle aged.

On the Road to Delphi

Tourist, beware.
The Sacred Bay
of Corinth
is charged
with aluminum;
at the Crossroads,
almost visible,
Oedipus waits.
Have an offering ready,
and a sacrifice.
You may ask
one question;
be specific.
The answer has always
been the same.
Look for it
among the broken stones
under your sandal
or in the unbroken light
of the Mediterranean sky.
And remember this:
virgins were said
to be unreliable,
so they chose as priestess
a woman of a certain age.
By the moon
your flesh is the color
of marble . . .
you are that age now.

Pain

More faithful
than lover or husband
it cleaves to you,
calling itself by your name
as if there had been a ceremony.

At night you turn and turn
searching for the one
bearable position,
but though you may finally sleep
it wakens ahead of you.

How heavy it is,
displacing with its volume
your very breath.
Before, you seemed to weigh nothing,
your arms might have been wings.

Now each finger adds its measure;
you are pulled down by the weight
of your own hair.
And if your life should disappear ahead of you
you would not run after it.

Weather Forecast

Somewhere it is about to snow,
if not in the northern suburbs,
then in the west,
if not there, then here.
And the wind
which is camouflaged now
by the perfect stillness of trees
will make some weathercock dizzy
with its fickle breath.
In the blood's failing heat
we wait for the verdict
of snow. You bite into an apple
with the sound boots make
crunching through
the first icy layers.
The whites of your eyes are cold.
The moons of your nails
are frozen mounds.
A single match striking
against the bottom of a shoe
is our only prayer.

blizzard

the snow
has forgotten
how to stop
it falls
stuttering
at the glass
a silk windsock
of snow
blowing
under the porch light
tangling trees
which bend
like old women
snarled
in their own
knitting
snow drifts
up to the step
over the doorsill
a pointillist's blur
the wedding
of form and motion
shaping itself
to the wish of
any object it touches
chairs become
laps of snow
the moon could be
breaking apart
and falling
over the eaves
over the roof
a white bear

shaking its paw
at the window
splitting the hive
of winter
snow stinging
the air
I pull a comforter
of snow
up to my chin
and tumble
to sleep
as the whole
alphabet
of silence
falls out of the
sky

There Are Poems

There are poems
that are never written,
that simply move across
the mind
like skywriting
on a still day:
slowly the first word
drifts west,
the last letters dissolve
on the tongue,
and what is left
is the pure blue
of insight, without cloud
or comfort.

Response

"a ban on the following subject
matter: the Holocaust, grand-
parents, Friday night candle light-
ing . . . Jerusalem at dusk."

from the poetry editor of *Response*

It is not dusk
in Jerusalem
it is simply morning

and the grandparents have disappeared
into the Holocaust
taking their sabbath candles with them.

Light your poems, hurry.
Already the sun is leaning
towards the west

though the grandparents and candles
have long since burned down
to stubs.

On Hearing the Testimony of
Those Revived After Cardiac Arrest

Wrenched back to life,
the door of death abruptly slammed
in their faces,
each mentions light
across that threshold
and someone once loved
waiting.

I think of Blake's Songs
Of Innocence; of God
and his lambs on a pediment of cloud;
of harps and incense.
Those candles snuffed out
by the cold thumb of reason
rekindle now:

they light up
pastures as rolling
as these Maryland hills;
my father practicing surgery
on an angel's wing;
the coin of metaphor spinning,
coming up Fact.

But long ago I chose
a purer sleep: no lamb
no tiger.

Presbyopia

The eye
defects first—
or is it the world
which takes the first step
backwards?
No matter.
Those blurred numerals
on the page
are tracks
to be followed
the rest of the way
alone.

Teeth

The date of death
is chiseled
on these rows of crumbling
headstones. Open!
Says God the dentist,
but who can solve
the mysteries
of the mouth,
its strict commandments?
The novocained jaw
grows heavy, more opulent
than speech.
Will its seeds scatter
like Indian corn
to sow our graves?
Will some chieftain dance,
a necklace of my teeth
circling his throat,
while elsewhere
my grandson's son sleeps,
a single tooth
hidden in the moist cave
of his mouth,
its milky light
the only candle
left?

You Who Are Literal

You who are literal even in love,
who treat each word
as journeyman to a fact,
consider the ambiguity of birds:
the owl's pentameter, for instance
the jay who names
his territories aloud—
you label those martial cries
song. And the weather:
the operatic fall of snow
buries alive with its grace notes
the roots of trees.
We are only translators, uneasy
unequipped.
In the hungry dawn
strange syllables stain our mouths
like berries picked deep
in the woods. Bitter or healing
poisonous or sweet
how are we to say?

My Achilles Son

My Achilles son
once clutched me
by the heel as I worked
to make myself
invulnerable.
Sulking
in the stove's half light
I bruised herbs,
watched dough heave itself
from bowls, rearranged
the dust—
and he at my feet.
Those fires
are salted down.
My hands remember only
the spell of wool:
I will cover the winter fields
with squares of knitting,
then lie down under them.
Nothing is left to happen.
Only his voice
still keeps me
like an arrow
from my proper rest,
pointing towards
the once dropped stitch,
the charred loaf,
the old disinheritance
of second sons.
Each time I lean
against the heavy shoulder
of sleep
a phone rings,

and from somewhere
I hear that voice—
then a buzz
on the line between us
from the whole
murderous hive
of possibilities.

Widow's Walk, Somewhere Inland

This landlocked house should grace a harbor:
its widow's walk of grey pickets
surveys an inland sea
of grass; wind
breaks like surf against
its rough shingles.

In summer the two grown sons
tie up here for awhile.
The daughter with her mermaid hair
sits on a rock; her legs will soon be long enough
to carry her away.

Sometimes the woman
lies awake
watching the fireflies bobbing
like ship's lights, the bats
with their strict radar
patrolling the dark.

The man will leave too,
one way or another,
sufficient as an old snail
carrying his small house
on his back.
She will remain, pacing

the widow's walk.
At dusk she'll pick the milky flowers
that grow by the porch stair;
she'll place them in the window,
each polished petal a star
for someone to steer home by.

25th Anniversary

There is something I want
to tell you beyond love
or gratitude or sex, beyond
irritation or a purer anger.
For years I have hoarded
your small faults the way
I might hoard kindling
towards some future conflagration,
and from the moment you broke
into my life, all out of breath,
I have half expected you
to break back out.
But here we are
like the married couple
from Cerveteri who smile
from their 6th-century sarcophagus
as if they are giving a party.
How young we were in Rome, buying
their portraits on postcards,
thinking that we too
were entangled already
beyond amputation, beyond
even death, as we are
as we are now.

Ethics

In ethics class so many years ago
our teacher asked this question every fall:
if there were a fire in a museum
which would you save, a Rembrandt painting
or an old woman who hadn't many
years left anyhow? Restless on hard chairs
caring little for pictures or old age
we'd opt one year for life, the next for art
and always half-heartedly. Sometimes
the woman borrowed my grandmother's face
leaving her usual kitchen to wander
some drafty, half-imagined museum.
One year, feeling clever, I replied
why not let the woman decide herself?
Linda, the teacher would report, eschews
the burdens of responsibility.
This fall in a real museum I stand
before a real Rembrandt, old woman,
or nearly so, myself. The colors
within this frame are darker than autumn,
darker even than winter—the browns of earth,
though earth's most radiant elements burn
through the canvas. I know now that woman
and painting and season are almost one
and all beyond saving by children.

At My Window

I have thought much
about snow,
the mute pilgrimage
of all those flakes
and about the dark wanderings
of leaves.

I have stalked
all four seasons
and seen how they beat
the same path
through the same woods
again and again.

I used to take a multitude
of trains, trusting
the strategy of tracks,
of distance.
I sailed on ships
trusting the arbitrary north.

Now I stand still
at my window
watching the snow
which knows only one direction,
falling in silence
towards silence.